I0731867

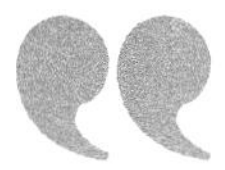

I know that sometimes I get scared
And make it up as I go along
There are days I get caught up in worry
And allow my fears to take over.

But what I'm learning
on this journey
is that I don't need to pause
for the tough feelings to pass
for me to be who I am to do my work.

And I am reminding myself
day after day that:
"I am **graced** to handle this".

Signed:

....

Created and published by Redefining Living
Creator of inspirational products for everyday brilliance at Redefiningliving.org
Nottingham - UK

ISBN: 978-1-8383923-2-1

AJI R. MICHAEL

FOR EVERYDAY BRILLIANCE

So, let's start here:

Have you ever painted a picture of how you want your career, relationships, health should look like, and the whole process is taking a toll on you?

Our 21st-century lives are in overdrive, filled with stress, headaches, deadlines and the constant struggle between who you are, who you want to be and who you were taught you should be.

You were taught to push and strive to be on top of your game. You must be attractive and intelligent, look professional but trendy, be well educated, healthy; the list goes on.

Consider this journal as your invitation to master the art of everyday brilliance.

The time of your pushing, forcing and trying to plan every detail of your life is over. Give that part of yourself a huge hug and ask them to sit down because they're no longer needed.

Beautiful things are about to emerge, situations that seem impossible are positively turning around for good, the beauty of this is that; it requires no effort from you.

This is the time for:

- Active Listening
- Waiting
- Trusting
- Receiving and
- Taking fewer but more inspired actions

An overview of the sections

Today I am..... ◆

Every day you will choose a state of your being, known as your "State of mind" - your "state of being" is the quality of your consciousness. When you're in control of your state of being, you're the master of your emotions; you understand that life is happening for you, not to you. For example, when was the last time you were in a bad mood? How did being in that state affect other parts of your life?

Your being influences your thinking, which affects your speaking, which causes doing, which puts in place the system to receive and experience what you created in your being and thinking.

In reality, you have the power to transform your state of being – and do so in an instant.

You can either do something to “be joyful,” or you can start your day by simply deciding to “be joyful.” Then the actions that you take will automatically reflect this. So, decide who you want to “be” (that is, what state of being you wish to experience), then move into that state, that is, be that person without doing anything.

On the last page of this journal, I have created a word cloud, states of Being that you may like to see expressed in you, as you, and through you. You can change your state of being at any time during the day. I’ll suggest you pick one state of being a day and repeat this for 21days. Though this process may sound strange at first, it requires practice so that your brain gets used to it. Affirmations and maintaining a healthy lifestyle will help you make the most of this process. My podcast: #10 self-care practices to get you back into alignment is a great place to start; Redefining Living Podcast is available on Apple podcast and Spotify.

My 3 commitments:

This section is where you write your fewer but more inspired actions. It is from your state of being that inspired actions will flow, then the doing. And whatever you ‘Do” will be a reflection of the state of being which gave it birth.

◆

For example, when you say: “Today I am Confident”, your inspired actions might be to complete a pending job application form, submit a proposal, make some business calls; you’ll be doing all of these actions from a state of “I am Confident”. Confident in yourself, your ability and that you are divinely inspired.

Your mind may tell you that these actions are too simple or not bring your desired result; that’s ok. Your mind will soon get used to it. Remarkable success in your business and career endeavours is a result of your being and not the other way around as most people do. Your ‘Being’ is your source – your identity. After all, you are a human ‘Being.’

Go and make it happen and above all, you’re graced to handle this.

Cheers to everyday brilliance!

Aji Michael
Founder, Redefining Living

Today I am

My 3 commitments:

1.

2.

3.

I am graced to handle this

For everyday brilliance

Today I am

My 3 commitments:

1.

2.

3.

I am graced to handle this

For everyday brilliance

Today I am

My 3 commitments:

1.

2.

3.

I am graced to handle this

For everyday brilliance

Today I am

My 3 commitments:

1.

2.

3.

I am graced to handle this

For everyday brilliance

Today I am

My 3 commitments:

1.

2.

3.

I am graced to handle this

For everyday brilliance

Today I am

My 3 commitments:

1.

2.

3.

I am graced to handle this

For everyday brilliance

Today I am

My 3 commitments:

1.

2.

3.

I am graced to handle this

For everyday brilliance

Today I am

My 3 commitments:

1.

2.

3.

I am graced to handle this

For everyday brilliance

Today I am

My 3 commitments:

1.

2.

3.

I am graced to handle this

For everyday brilliance

Today I am

My 3 commitments:

1.

2.

3.

I am graced to handle this

For everyday brilliance

Today I am

My 3 commitments:

1.

2.

3.

I am graced to handle this

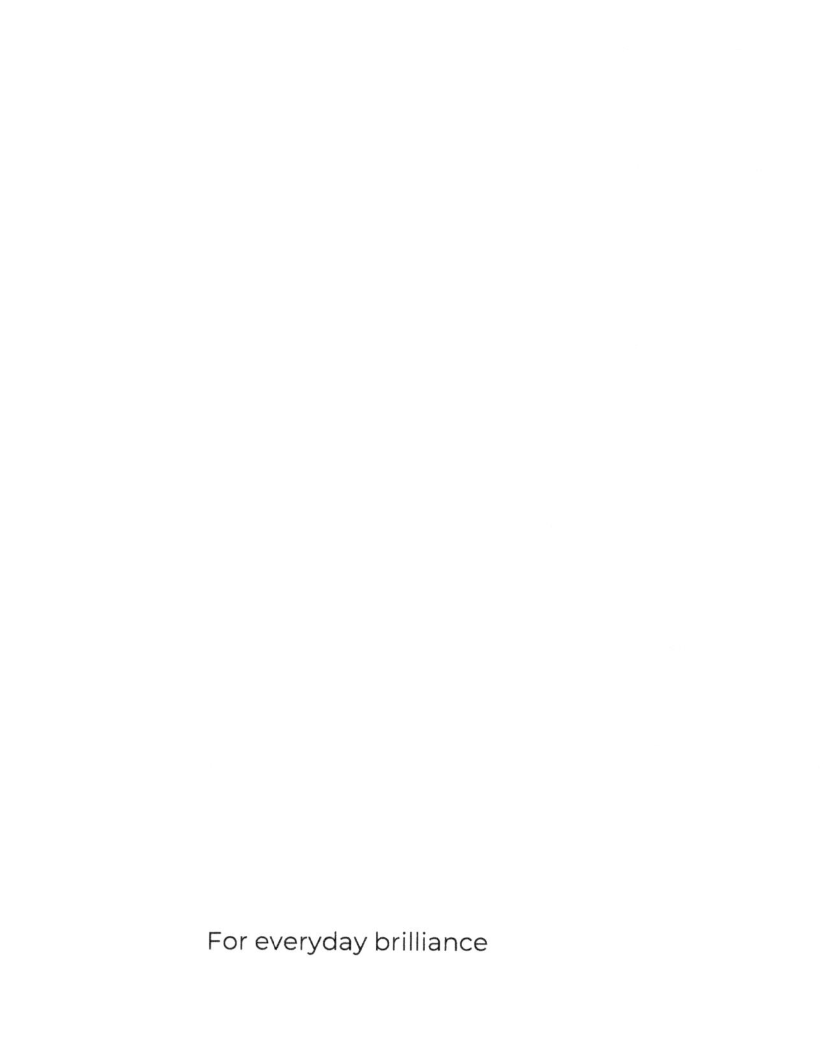

For everyday brilliance

Today I am

My 3 commitments:

1.

2.

3.

I am graced to handle this

For everyday brilliance

Today I am

My 3 commitments:

1.

2.

3.

I am graced to handle this

For everyday brilliance

Today I am

My 3 commitments:

1.

2.

3.

I am graced to handle this

For everyday brilliance

Today I am

My 3 commitments:

1.

2.

3.

I am graced to handle this

For everyday brilliance

Today I am

My 3 commitments:

1.

2.

3.

I am graced to handle this

For everyday brilliance

Today I am

My 3 commitments:

1.

2.

3.

I am graced to handle this

For everyday brilliance

Today I am

My 3 commitments:

1.

2.

3.

I am graced to handle this

Today I am

My 3 commitments:

1.

2.

3.

For everyday brilliance

Today I am

My 3 commitments:

1.

2.

3.

I am graced to handle this

For everyday brilliance

Today I am

My 3 commitments:

1.

2.

3.

For everyday brilliance

Today I am

My 3 commitments:

1.

2.

3.

I am graced to handle this

Today I am

My 3 commitments:

1.

2.

3.

I am graced to handle this

For everyday brilliance

Today I am

My 3 commitments:

1.

2.

3.

I am graced to handle this

For everyday brilliance

Today I am

My 3 commitments:

1.

2.

3.

I am graced to handle this

For everyday brilliance

Today I am

My 3 commitments:

1.

2.

3.

I am graced to handle this

For everyday brilliance

Today I am

My 3 commitments:

1.

2.

3.

I am graced to handle this

For everyday brilliance

Today I am

My 3 commitments:

1.

2.

3.

I am graced to handle this

For everyday brilliance

Today I am

My 3 commitments:

1.

2.

3.

I am graced to handle this

For everyday brilliance

Today I am

My 3 commitments:

1.

2.

3.

I am graced to handle this

For everyday brilliance

Today I am

My 3 commitments:

1.

2.

3.

I am graced to handle this

For everyday brilliance

Today I am

My 3 commitments:

1.

2.

3.

I am graced to handle this

Today I am

My 3 commitments:

1.

2.

3.

For everyday brilliance

Today I am

My 3 commitments:

1.

2.

3.

For everyday brilliance

Today I am

My 3 commitments:

1.

2.

3.

I am graced to handle this

Today I am

My 3 commitments:

1.

2.

3.

I am graced to handle this

Today I am

My 3 commitments:

1.

2.

3.

I am graced to handle this

For everyday brilliance

Today I am

My 3 commitments:

1.

2.

3.

I am graced to handle this

For everyday brilliance

Today I am

My 3 commitments:

1.

2.

3.

I am graced to handle this

Today I am

Considerate
Happy
Faithful
Peaceful
Creative Patient Fun
Compassionate
Goodness Love Kind Sensual
Classy
Forgiving
Elegant Wise
Generous
Gracious
Caring
Joyful
Merciful
Enough
Beautiful

For everyday brilliance

www.ingramcontent.com/pod-product-compliance
Lightning Source LLC
Chambersburg PA
CBHW072011210726
48294CB00013B/1989

* 9 7 8 1 8 3 8 3 9 2 3 2 1 *